The Path of Power

Henri J. M. Nouwen

The Path of Power

CROSSROAD • NEW YORK

1995

The Crossroad Publishing Company
370 Lexington Avenue, New York, NY 10017

Copyright © 1995 by Henri J. M. Nouwen

Printed in the United States of America

ISBN 0-8245-2003-3

S ITTING IN A PLANE and looking down on the broad landscapes — the rivers, lakes, and mountains — and seeing the winding roads and little villages spread out over the earth, you wonder why it is so hard for people to live peacefully together. The astronauts seeing our blue planet from their space shuttle were so overwhelmed by its beauty that it seemed impossible for them to believe that its inhabitants were busy destroying their own home and killing each other through war and exploitation.

Distance sometimes helps us to get a sharper vision of our human condition and to raise some very good critical questions!

I too want to take a look at our

world from a distance, not from the physical distance of a plane or a space vehicle, but from the spiritual distance of our faith. I want to look at us, human beings, from above, with the eyes of God. Jesus always looked at the human condition from above and tried to teach us to look as he did. "I come from above," he said, "and I want you to be reborn from above so that you will be able to see with new eyes."

This is what theology is all about. It is looking at reality with the eyes of God. There is so much to look at: land and sky; sun, stars, and moon; women, men, and children; continents, countries, cities and towns, and countless very specific issues in the past, present, and future. And that's why there are so many "theologies." The sacred Scriptures help us to look at the rich variety of all that is with the eyes of God and so discern the ways to live.

I want to offer in this little book a theology of weakness. I want to look

with God's eyes at our experience of brokenness, limitedness, woundedness, and frailty in a way that Jesus taught us in the hope that such a vision will offer us a safe way to travel on earth. I will focus on three words: "power," "powerlessness," and "power." I first want to explore the power that oppresses and destroys. Then I want to show how that power is disarmed through powerlessness, and finally I want to proclaim the true power that liberates, reconciles, and heals.

Power

I. When God looks at our world, God weeps. God weeps because the lust for power has entrapped and corrupted the human spirit. Instead of gratitude there is resentment, instead of praise there is criticism, instead of forgiveness there is revenge, instead of healing there is wounding, instead of compassion there is competition, instead of cooperation there is violence, and instead of love there is immense fear.

God weeps when God looks at our beautiful planet and sees thousands of maimed bodies lying on the battlefields, lonely children roaming the streets of big cities, prisoners locked behind bars and thick walls, mentally ill men and women wasting their time in the wards of large institutions, and millions of people dying from starvation and neglect. God weeps because God knows the agony and anguish we have brought upon ourselves by wanting to take our destiny in our own hands and lord it over others.

When we look around and within us with the eyes of God, it is not hard to see the all-pervading lust for power. Why are Serbs killing Moslems? Why are Protestants and Catholics throwing bombs at each other? Why was the president of Sri Lanka murdered, the prime minister of Belgium kidnapped, and why did the political leader of France commit suicide?

Let's look into our own hearts! Aren't we constantly concerned with whether we are noticed or not, appreciated or not, rewarded or not? Aren't we always asking ourselves whether we are better or worse, stronger or weaker, faster or slower than the one who stands beside us? Haven't we, from elementary school on, experienced most of our fellow human beings as rivals in the race for success, influence, and popularity? And... aren't we so insecure about who we are that we will grab any, yes any, form of power that gives us a little bit of control over who we are, what we do, and where we go?

When we are willing to look at things through God's eyes, we soon will see that what is happening in Bosnia, South Africa, Ireland, or Los Angeles is not so far away from our own hearts. As soon as our own safety is threatened we grab for the first stick or gun available and we say that *our* survival is what really counts, even when thousands of others are not going to make it.

I know my sticks and guns! Sometimes it is a friend with more influence than I, sometimes it is money or a degree, sometimes it is a little talent that others don't have, and sometimes it is a special knowledge, or a hidden memory, or even a cold stare...and I will grab it quickly and without much hesitation when I need it to stay in control. Before I fully realize it I have pushed my friends away.

God looks at us and weeps because wherever we use power to give us a sense of self, we separate from God and each other, and our lives become *diabolic,* in the literal meaning of that word: *divisive.*

II. But there is something worse than economic and political power. It is religious power. When God looks at our world, God not only weeps but is also angry — angry because many of those who pray, offer praise, and call out to God, "Lord, Lord!" are also corrupted by power. In anger God says:

"These people honor me only with lip service, while their hearts are far from me. Their reverence of me is worthless; the lessons they teach are nothing but human commandments" (Isa. 29:13).

The most insidious, divisive, and wounding power is the power used in the service of God. I am overwhelmed by the number of people who "have been wounded by religion." An unfriendly word by a minister or priest, a critical remark in church about a certain lifestyle, a refusal to welcome people at the table, an absence during an illness or death, and countless other hurts often remain longer in people's memories than other more world-like rejections. Thousands of separated and divorced men and women, numerous

*"These people honor me
only with lip service,
while their hearts
are far from me."*

(ISA. 29:13)

gay and lesbian people, and all of the homeless people who felt unwelcome in the houses of worship of their brothers and sisters in the human family have turned away from God because they experienced the use of power when they expected an expression of love.

The devastating influence of power in the hands of God's people becomes very clear when we think of the crusades, the pogroms, the policies of apartheid, and the long history of religious wars up to these very days, but it might be harder to realize that many contemporary religious movements create the fertile soil for these immense human tragedies to happen again.

In these days of great economic and political uncertainty, one of the greatest temptations is to use our faith as a way to exercise power over others and thereby supplant God's commandments with human commandments.

It is easy to understand why so many people have turned away in disgust from anything vaguely connected with religion. When power is used to proclaim good news, good news very soon becomes bad, very bad news. And that's what makes God angry.

But God looks at our world not only with sad and angry eyes; God's mercy is far greater than God's sadness and anger. As the Psalmist says: "God's anger lasts but a moment" (Ps. 30:5). In an all-embracing mercy God

*In Jesus of Nazareth,
the powerless God
appeared among us
to unmask the illusion
of power.*

chooses to disarm the power of evil through powerlessness — God's own powerlessness.

Powerlessness

I. What was and is God's response to the diabolic power that rules the world and destroys the people and their land? God chose powerlessness. God chose to enter into human history in complete weakness. That divine choice forms the center of the Christian faith. In Jesus of Nazareth, the powerless God appeared among us to unmask the illusion of power, to disarm the prince of darkness who rules the world, and to bring the divided human race to a new unity. It is through total and unmitigated powerlessness that God shows us divine mercy. The radical, divine choice is the choice to reveal glory, beauty, truth, peace, joy, and, most of all, love in and through the complete divestment of power. It is very hard — if not impossible — for us to grasp this divine mystery. We keep praying to the "Almighty and powerful God," but all might and power is absent from the one who reveals God to us saying: "When you see me you see the Father." If we truly want to love God, we have to look at the man of Nazareth whose life was wrapped in weakness. And his weakness opens for us the way to the heart of God.

People with power do not invite intimacy. We fear people with power.

They can control us and force us to do what we don't want to do. We look up to people with power. They have what we do not have and can give or refuse to give, according to their will. We envy people with power. They can afford to go where we cannot go and do what we cannot do. But God does not want us to be afraid, distant, or envious. God wants to come close, very close, so close that we can rest in the intimacy of God as children in their mother's arms.

Therefore God became a little baby. Who can be afraid of a little baby? A tiny little baby is completely dependent on its parents, nurses, and caregivers. Yes, God wanted to become so powerless that he could not eat or drink, walk or talk, play or work without many people's help. Yes, God became dependent on human beings to grow up and live among us and proclaim the good news. Yes, indeed, God chose to become so powerless that the realization of God's own mission among us became completely dependent on us. How can you fear a baby you rock in your arms, how can you look up to a baby that is so little and fragile, how can you be envious of a baby who only smiles at you in response to your tenderness? That's the mystery of the incarnation. God became human, in no way different from other human beings, to break through the walls of power in total weakness. That's the story of Jesus.

And how did that story end? On a cross, where the same human person hangs naked with nails through his hands and feet. The powerlessness of the manger has become the powerlessness of the cross. People jeer at him, laugh at him, spit in his face, and shout: "He saved others; he cannot save himself! He is the King of Israel; let him come down from the cross now, and we will believe in him" (Matt. 27:42). He hangs there, his flesh torn apart by lead-filled whips, his heart broken by the rejection of his friends and abuse from his enemies, his mind tortured by anguish, his spirit shrouded in

God became human,
in no way different
from other human beings,
to break through
the walls of power
in total weakness.

the darkness of abandonment — total weakness, total powerlessness. That's how God chose to reveal to us the divine love, bring us back into an embrace of compassion, and convince us that anger has been melted away in endless mercy.

II. But there is more to be said about God's powerlessness as it is revealed in Jesus of Nazareth. There is not only a powerless birth and a powerless death, but — strange as it may seem — a powerless life.

Jesus, the powerless child of God, is blessed in powerlessness. When, after a long hidden life in Nazareth, Jesus begins his ministry, he first offers us a self-portrait. "Blessed are the poor," he said. Jesus is poor, not in control, but marginal in his society. What good can come from Nazareth?

"Blessed are the gentle," he said. Jesus does not break the bruised reed. He always cares for the little ones.

"Blessed are those who mourn," he said. Jesus does not hide his grief, but lets his tears flow when his friend dies and when he foresees the destruction of his beloved Jerusalem.

"Blessed are those who hunger and thirst for justice," he said. Jesus doesn't hesitate to criticize injustice and to defend the hungry, the dying, and the lepers.

"Blessed are the merciful," he said. Jesus doesn't call for revenge but heals always and everywhere.

"Blessed are the pure in heart," he said. Jesus remains focused only on what is necessary and does not allow his attention to be divided by many distractions.

"Blessed are the peacemakers," he said. Jesus does not stress differences, but reconciles people as brothers and sisters in one family.

"Blessed are those who are persecuted," he said. Jesus does not expect success and popularity, but knows that rejections and abandonment will make him suffer.

The Beatitudes give us Jesus' self-portrait. It is the portrait of the powerless God. It is also the portrait we glimpse wherever we see the sick, the prisoners, the refugees, the lonely, the victims of sexual abuse, the people with AIDS, and the dying. It is through their powerlessness that we are called to become brothers and sisters. It is through their powerlessness that we are called to deepen our bonds of friendship and love. It is through their powerlessness that we are challenged to lay down our weapons, offer each other forgiveness, and make peace. And it is through their powerlessness that we are constantly reminded of Jesus' words: "You foolish people, is it not necessary to suffer and so enter into glory?" Indeed, God's powerlessness and the powerlessness of the human race of which God became part has become the door to the house of love.

Power

I. Our world is ruled by diabolic powers that divide and destroy. In and through the powerless Jesus, God disarmed these powers. However, this mystery confronts us with a new and very hard question: how to live in this world as witnesses to a powerless God and build the Kingdom of love and peace?

Does powerlessness mean that we are doomed to be doormats for our power-hungry society? Does it mean that it is good to be soft, passive, subservient — always allowing the powers of darkness to dominate our lives? Does it mean that economic weakness, organizational weakness, physical and

*"My strength
is made perfect
in weakness."*

(2 COR. 12:9)

emotional weakness have now, suddenly, become virtues? Does it mean that people who are poorly educated, poorly organized, and poorly prepared for their tasks can now brag about their poverty as a blessing that calls for gratitude? When we read Paul's words: "My strength is made perfect in weakness" (2 Cor. 12:9), do you imagine that we are dealing with a weakling who uses his low self-esteem as an argument to proclaim the gospel?

We touch here on one of the most dangerous traps of a theology of weakness. When we can become free from the enslaving powers of the world only by being enslaved by weakness, it seems a lot better to stay on the side of Satan than on the side of God. If a theology of weakness becomes a theology for weaklings, then such a theology is a comfortable excuse for incompetence, submissiveness, self-denigration, and defeat in all fields!

This is far from a theoretical possibility. Not seldom is financial, intellectual, and spiritual weakness interpreted as a divine privilege; not seldom is competent medical or psychological help delayed or avoided in the conviction that it is better to suffer for God than not to suffer; not seldom is careful planning, aggressive fundraising, and intelligent strategizing for the future frowned on as a lack of faithfulness to the ideal of powerlessness. Not seldom have the sick, the poor, the handicapped, and all those who suffer been romanticized as God's privileged children, without much support to free them from their fate.

Nietzsche rightly criticized a theology of weakness. For him it was a theology that kept the poor in their poverty and gave the rulers of the religious establishment a chance to keep their "faithful" in a state of subservient obedience. Indeed, there is a spirituality of powerlessness, of weakness, of littleness that can be extremely dangerous, especially in the hands of those who feel they are called to speak and to act in God's name. Of them, Jesus says: "They tie up heavy burdens and lay them on people's shoulders, but they will not lift a finger to move them" (Matt. 23:4).

A theology of weakness challenges us to look at weakness not as a worldly weakness that allows us to be manipulated by the powerful in society and church, but as a total and unconditional dependence on God that opens us to be true channels of the divine power that heals the wounds of humanity and renews the face of the earth. The theology of weakness claims power, God's power, the all-transforming power of love.

Indeed, a theology of weakness is a theology that shows a God weeping for the human race entangled in its power games and angry that these same power games are so greedily used by so-called religious people. Indeed a theology of weakness is a theology that shows how God unmasks the power games of the world and the church by entering into history in complete powerlessness. But a theology of weakness wants, ultimately, to show that God offers us, human beings, the divine power to walk on the earth confidently with heads erect.

II. God is powerful. Jesus doesn't hesitate to speak about God's power. He says: "In truth I tell you, there are some standing here who will not taste death before they see the kingdom of God come with power" (Matt. 9:2). Wherever Jesus went there was the experience of divine power. Luke writes: "Everyone in the crowd was trying to touch him because power came out of him that cured them all" (Luke 6:19). When a woman who had suffered from a hemorrhage for twelve years touched the fringe of Jesus' cloak, trusting that Jesus would cure her, Jesus said: "Someone touched me, I felt that power had gone out from me" (Luke 8:46). Jesus was filled with God's power. Jesus claims for himself the power to forgive sins, the power to heal, the power to call to life, yes, all power. The final words he directs to his friends are full of this conviction. He says: "All power in heaven and on earth has been given to me. Go, therefore, make disciples of all nations" (Matt. 29:12–19).

Power is claimed, and power is given. In and through the powerless

Jesus, God wants to empower us, give us the power that Jesus had, and send us out — to cast out demons, to heal the sick, to call the dead to life, to reconcile the estranged, to create community and to build the Kingdom of God.

A theology of weakness is a theology of divine empowering. It is not a theology for weaklings but a theology for men and women who claim for themselves the power of love that frees them from fear and enables them to put their light on the lampstands and do the work of the Kingdom.

Yes, we are poor, gentle, mourning, hungry and thirsty for justice, merciful, pure of heart, peacemakers, and always persecuted by a hostile world. But no weaklings, no doormats. The Kingdom of heaven is ours, the earth our inheritance. We are comforted, have our fill, experience mercy, are recognized as God's children and . . . see God. That's power, real power, power that comes from above.

The movement from power to power through powerlessness is what we are called to. As fearful, anxious, insecure, and wounded people we are tempted constantly to grab the little bit of power that the world around us offers, left and right, here and there, now and then. These bits of power make us little puppets jerked up and down on strings until we are dead. But insofar as we dare to be baptized in powerlessness, always moving toward the poor who have no such power, we will be plunged right into the heart of God's endless mercy. We will be free to re-enter our world with the same divine power with which Jesus came and be able to walk in the valley of darkness and tears, unceasingly in communion with God, with our heads erect, confidently standing under the cross of our life.

It is this power that engenders leaders for our communities, women and men who dare to take risks and take new initiatives. It is this power that enables us to be not only gentle as doves, but also as clever as serpents in our dealings with governments and church agencies. It is this power that enables us to talk straight and without hesitation about money with people who have financial resources, to call men and woman to radical service, to challenge people to make a long-term commitment, and to keep announcing the good news everywhere at all times. It is this divine power that makes us saints — fearless — who can make all things new.

Conclusion

Are there any disciplines to keep us moving from dividing power to uniting power, from destructive power to healing power, from paralyzing power to enabling power?

Let me suggest three, all of them disciplines to make us look from above with the eyes of God.

The first discipline is to focus always on the poor in this world. We must keep asking ourselves: "Where are the men, women, and children who are waiting for us to reach out to them?" Poverty in all its forms, physical, intellectual, and emotional, is not decreasing. To the contrary, the poor are everywhere around us — more

than ever. As the powers of darkness
show their hideous intentions with in-
creasing crudeness, the weeping of the
poor becomes louder and louder and
their misery more and more visible. We
have to keep listening, we have to keep
looking.

The second discipline is to trust that
God will truly care for the poor that
are given to us. We will have the financial, emotional, and physical support
we need, when we need it, and to the
degree that we need it. I am convinced
that there is a large body of people
ready to help with money, time, and
talent. But that body will remain invis-
ible unless we dare to take new risks.
If we want to have all our bases cov-
ered before we move to action, nothing

Be surprised by joy;
be surprised by the little
  flower
that shows its beauty
in the midst of a barren
  desert.

exciting will happen, but if we dare to take a few crazy risks because God asks us to do so, many doors that we didn't even know existed will be opened for us.

The third discipline is the hardest one. It is the discipline to be surprised not by suffering but by joy. As we grow old, we will have to stretch out our arms, be guided and led to places we would rather not go. What was true for Peter will be true for us. There is suffering ahead of us, immense suffering, a suffering that will continue to tempt us to think that we have chosen the wrong road and that others were more shrewd than we. But don't be surprised by pain. Be surprised by joy, be surprised by the little flower that shows its beauty in the

midst of a barren desert, and be surprised by the immense healing power
that keeps bursting forth like springs of
fresh water from the depth of our pain.

And so, with an eye focused on the
poor, a heart trusting that we will get
what we need, and a spirit always surprised by joy, we will be truly powerful
and walk through this valley of darkness performing miracles because it's
God's power that will go out from
us wherever we go and whomever we
meet.

Let me conclude with a little story
about John and Sandy. John and Sandy
are two very simple people. We all have
Johns and Sandys among us. One day
John said to Sandy: "We have never
had an argument. Let us have an ar-

gument like other people have." Sandy asked: "But how can we start an argument?" John answered: "It is very simple. I take a brick and say: 'It is mine,' and then you say: 'No it is mine,' and then we have an argument." So they sat down and John took a brick and said: "This brick is mine." Sandy looked gently at him and said: "Well, if it is yours take it." And so they could not have an argument.*

As long as we keep bricks in our hands and speak about mine and thine, our little power games gradually will escalate into big power games, and our big power games will lead to hatred, violence, and war. Looking at life from

*This story is an adaptation of a story from the desert fathers.

below, our fears and insecurities lead us to grab bricks wherever we can. But when we dare to let go of our bricks, empty our hands, and raise them up to the One who is our true refuge and our true stronghold, our poverty opens us to receive power from above, power that heals, power that will be a true blessing for ourselves and our world.

HENRI J. M. NOUWEN, author of more than thirty books, including *The Return of the Prodigal Son, Life of the Beloved, In the Name of Jesus,* and *Our Greatest Gift,* has taught at the University of Notre Dame, Yale, and Harvard. For the last seven years, he has shared his life with people with mental handicaps, as pastor of the l'Arche Daybreak community in Toronto, Canada.

Other books in *The Path* series